snapshot·picture·library

UNDERWATER ANIMALS

snapshot•picture•library

UNDERWATER ANIMALS

FOG CITY PRESS

Published by Fog City Press,
a division of Weldon Owen Inc.
415 Jackson Street
San Francisco, CA 94111
www.weldonowen.com

WELDON OWEN GROUP
Chief Executive Officer John Owen

WELDON OWEN INC.
President, Chief Executive Officer Terry Newell
Vice President, International Sales Stuart Laurence
Vice President, Sales and New Business Development Amy Kaneko
Vice President, Sales—Asia and Latin America Dawn Low
Vice President, Publisher Roger Shaw
Vice President, Creative Director Gaye Allen
Managing Editor, Fog City Press Karen Perez
Assistant Editor Sonia Vallabh
Art Director Bret Hansen
Designer Andreas Schueller
Design Assistant Kevin Yuen
Production Director Chris Hemesath
Production Manager Michelle Duggan
Color Manager Teri Bell

Text Sonia Vallabh
Introduction Barbara Vivian Rogers
Picture Research Kenneth McCue

A WELDON OWEN PRODUCTION
© 2008 Weldon Owen Inc.

Library of Congress Catalog-in-Publication
data is available upon request.

ISBN-13: 978-1-74089-748-8

10 9 8 7 6 5 4 3 2

Color separations by San Choy International, Singapore.
Printed by Tien Wah Press in Singapore.

From shallow coral reefs
to deep murky trenches,
the ocean offers an
underwater realm that's
home to remarkable
creatures and plants.

Even more amazing are the
ocean's forests of plankton
made up of tiny plants—that
produce half the oxygen we
breathe—and animals.

The ocean covers nearly
three-fourths of our planet's
surface. Maybe we should
really call it Planet Ocean!

Underwater
animals come
in all shapes
and sizes.

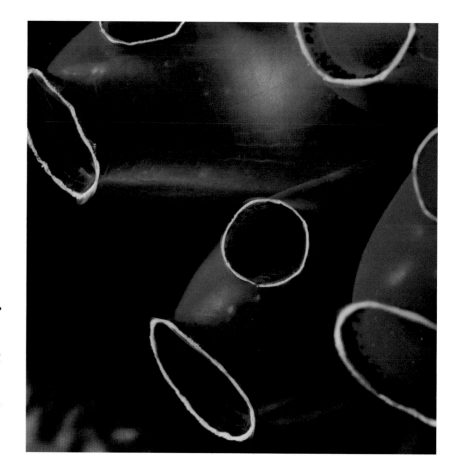

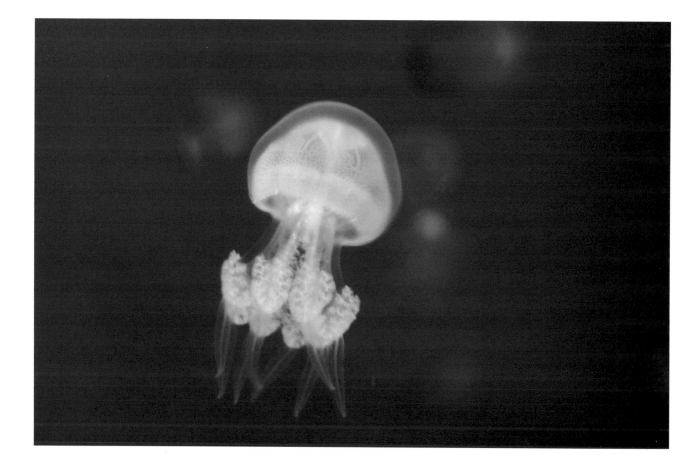

Orcas, sea turtles, and whale sharks are among the large creatures that glide through the ocean.

But look closely, and you can find all sorts of tiny animals too, such as this spotted cleaner shrimp.

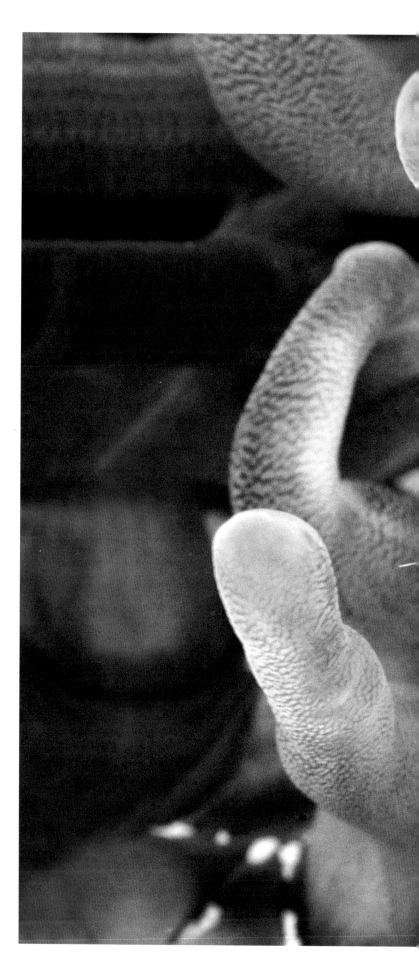

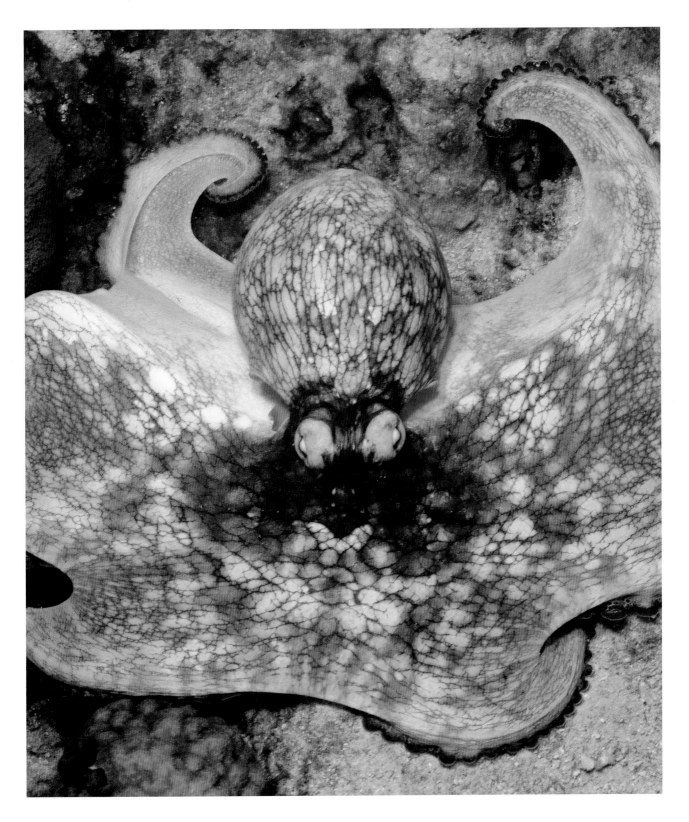

Some sea animals, such as starfish and octopuses, have long, swirling arms.

Anemones look like flowers, but they are animals! When little fish get too close, the anemones gobble them up.

The ocean is home to many brightly colored creatures.

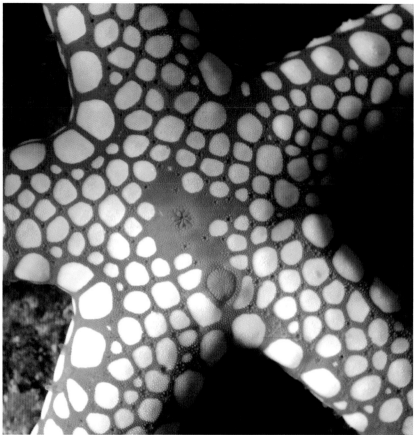

Most of them live on the continental shelf, the part of the ocean closest to land.

Some underwater animals are colored to blend into their habitats.

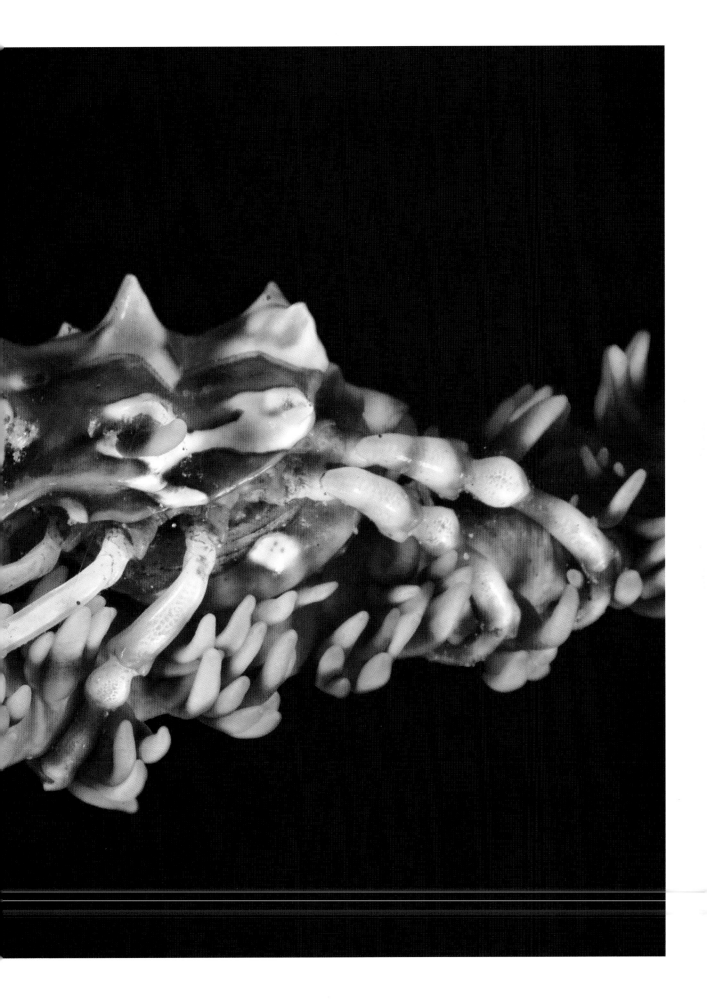

Camouflage
helps animals
hide from
predators.
Sometimes
it helps them
hide from
prey…until
it's too late!

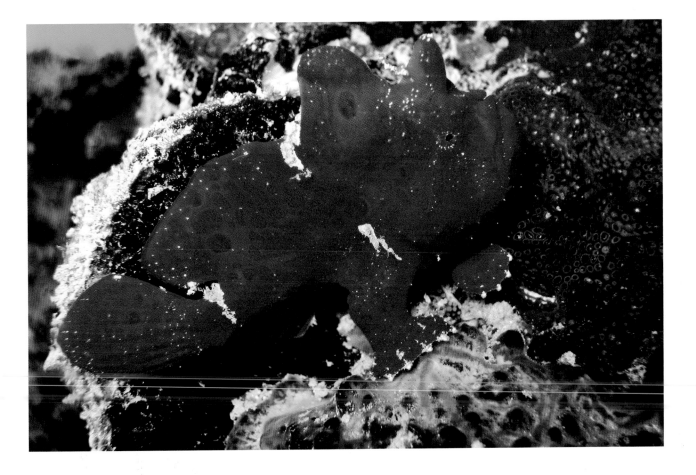

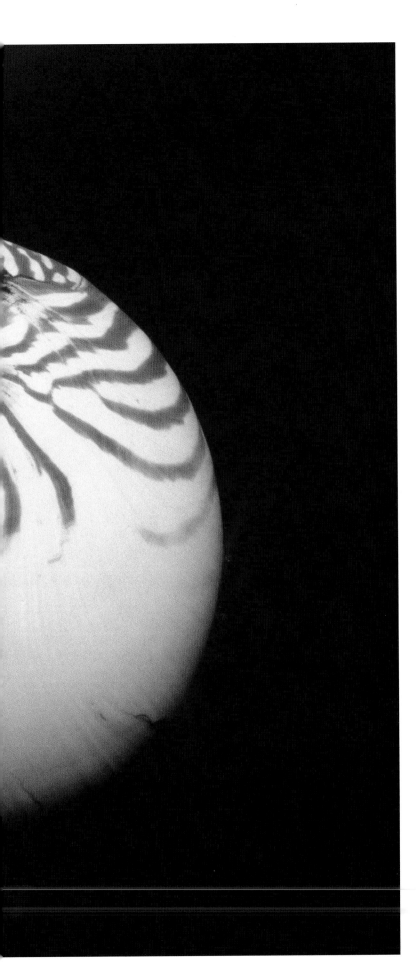

Many ocean
creatures look
like no other
animals on Earth.

Some don't even look like animals. Instead, they may look like rocks, plants…or even spaceships!

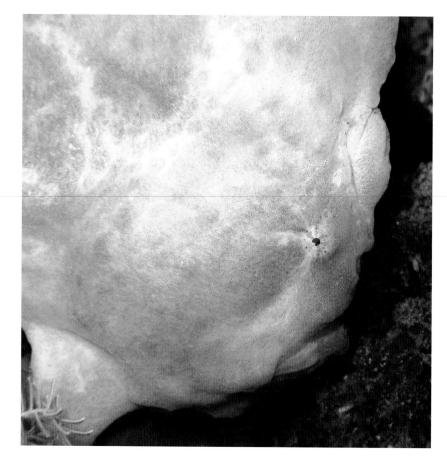

This animal
may look like
a pincushion,
but it's actually
a sea urchin.

Underwater creatures are not always friendly—some must know how to fight to survive.

Octopuses squirt ink at their enemies. They have also been known to fight small sharks…and win!

Jellyfish may
be beautiful,
but their
tentacles often
contain poison
that will sting
if it touches
your skin.

Jellyfish can't control which way they move—they mostly just float with the current—and yet, some are poisonous enough to kill you.

Crabs, which may seem small
and harmless under their shells,
are armed with pinching claws.

Horseshoe crabs can grow to be up to two feet long! Surprisingly, these creatures are more closely related to spiders than to crabs.

With so many hidden dangers,
the ocean might make you want
to run away and hide!

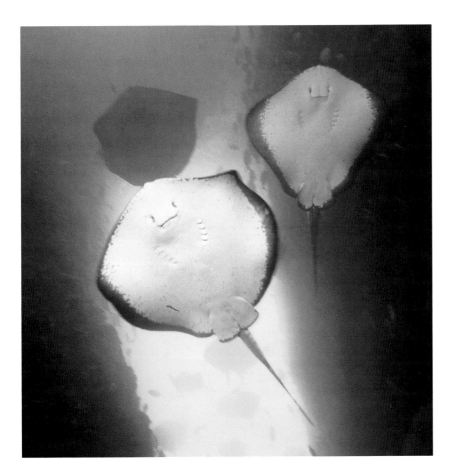

And yet, the ocean can be such a beautiful and peaceful place.

Some of the ocean's largest animals aren't very dangerous at all. Whale sharks eat only microscopic plankton and some small fish.

Whales eat plankton, too. It's amazing that such large animals can survive on a diet of tiny creatures.

Plankton spend
their lives drifting
wherever the
water takes them.
Other sea creatures
would rather hang
out at home on
the sea floor or in
a big seashell.

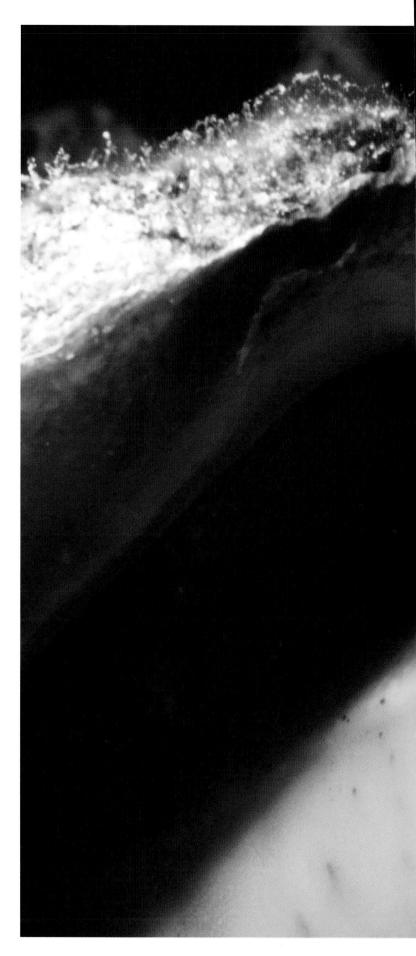

Just like us, ocean animals can often be found hanging out together.

The ocean is
the one habitat
on Earth where
humans do not
live. Perhaps this
is what makes it so
fascinating to us.

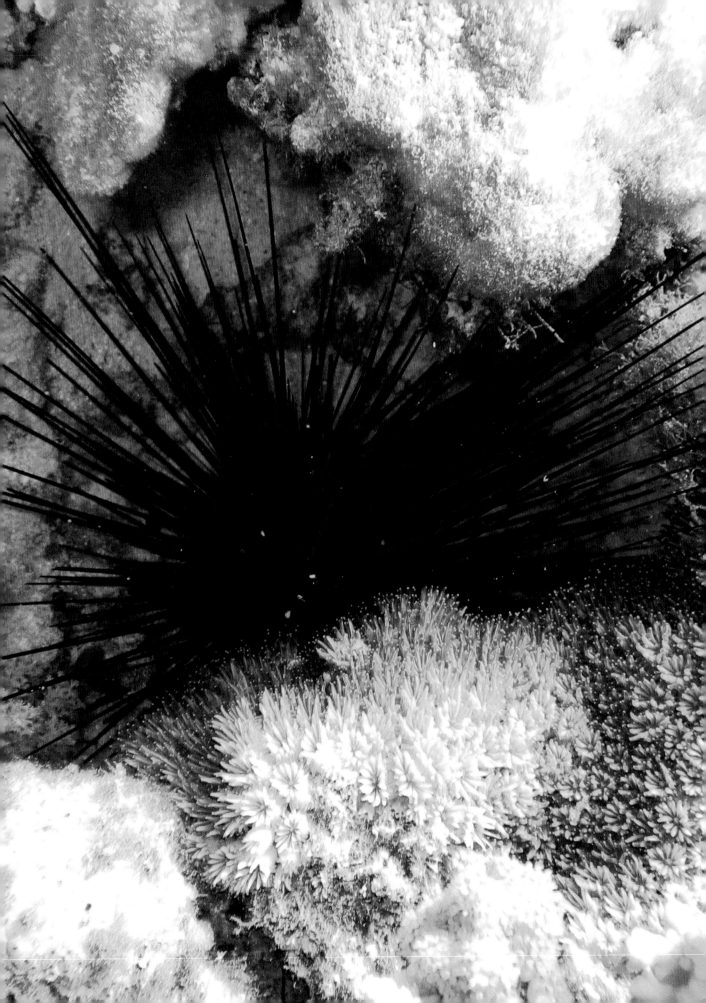

Luckily, we can visit and meet some of the amazing animals that live here.

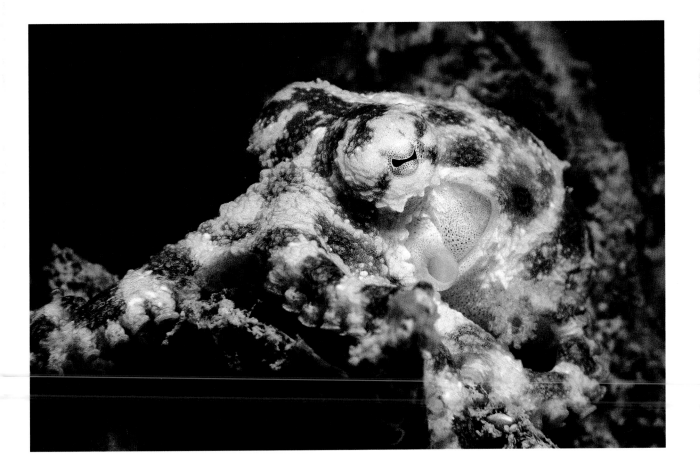

What a mysterious
place to explore!

Beluga Whale

 Starfish

 Sea Turtle

 Starfish

Caribbean Octopus

Decorator Crab

 Jellyfish

Feather Duster

Red Frogfish

 Soft Coral

Tube Anemone

Nautilus

 Jellyfish

 Feather Duster

 White Frogfish

    Tube Anemone

 Golden Tail Moray

Leafy Sea Dragon

 Orca Whale

Sea Star

Moon Jellyfish

 Sea Turtle

 Nudibranch

Sea Urchin

 Whale Sharks

 Sea Urchin

Coconut Octopus

 Spotted Cleaner Shrimp

 Camouflage Spider Crab

  Spider Crab

Octopus

 Lined Seahorse

 Seahorses

 Octopus

 Sea Turtle

 Jellyfish

 Moon Jellyfish

 Stingray

 Starfish

 Pacific Moon Jellyfish

 Coral

 Sea Urchin

 Jellyfish

 Whale Shark

Blue-Spotted Stingray

 Jellyfish

 Whale

Blue-Ringed Octopus

 Horseshoe Crab

 Minke Whales

Sea Turtle

 Red-Spotted Coral Crab

Beluga Whales

Mantis Shrimp

 Horseshoe Crab

 Queen Conch

 Moray Eel

 Dolphins

ACKNOWLEDGMENTS

Weldon Owen would like to thank the following people for their assistance in the production of this book: Lucie Parker, Phil Paulick, and Heather Stewart.

CREDITS